LEADERSHIP HERO CODE

LEADERSHIP HERO CODE

SEVEN PRINCIPLES
FOR THRIVING IN TODAY'S WORKPLACE

KRISTEN HEMINGWAY

HEMINGWAY
STRATEGIES
PUBLISHING

CHICAGO

Leadership Hero Code
Copyright © 2020 Kristen Hemingway

ISBN 978-0-578-58839-1

All rights reserved. No part of this book may be reproduced in any form on by an electronic or mechanical means, including information storage and retrieval systems, without permission in writing from the publisher, except by a reviewer who may quote brief passages in a review.

www.hemingwaystrategies.com

Book cover and interior designed by Christine M. Scott, Clever Crow Consulting and Design | clevercrow.com

For Dylan, an emerging, heart-centered leader, and my beloved change agent. For the TTHs and GSHs who hold space for my unique journey beyond the status quo. For HLC, my confidante and cheerleader. For SHB, my "yes, and" partner.

CONTENTS

PROLOGUE: The Price We Pay 9

CHAPTER 1: The Desire for More 13

CHAPTER 2: Three Principles for Personal Leadership Health 23

CHAPTER 3: Personal Principle #1 – Your Energy Bank 27

CHAPTER 4: Personal Principle #2 – Sense of Purpose 35

CHAPTER 5: Personal Principle #3 – Attention to Self-Care 43

CHAPTER 6: Four Principles for Team Leadership Health 51

CHAPTER 7: Team Principle #1 – Collective Energy 55

CHAPTER 8: Team Principle #2 – Psychological Safety 63

CHAPTER 9: Team Principle #3 – Authentic Exchanges 71

CHAPTER 10: Team Principle #4 – Vital Conversations 81

CHAPTER 11: Linking Leadership Principles to Purpose 89

CHAPTER 12: Integrating Personal and Team Leadership Principles ... 97

CHAPTER 13: Moving Your Team Into Action 105

BONUS EXPERIMENTS 113

END NOTES 119

ABOUT THE AUTHOR 123

PROLOGUE:
THE PRICE WE PAY

Memorial Day weekend is coming to a close. Pete has been happily basking in the glory of three days off work and the official arrival of summer. However, about 8pm, his inbox begins to swell. Pete is part of an eight-billion-dollar healthcare organization and the Chief Marketing Officer is sending panicky emails about Finance's decision to halt all incremental spending. Pete and his team have been relying on regular approval of millions of dollars of funding to cover their operating costs and all the "new initiatives" that get thrown their way. But this time, funding was denied. Imagining slash and burn of projects, paid media contracts and outside consultants means Pete did not sleep satisfactorily that night.

The week ahead is full of trade-off discussions and "hold" conversations. By the time Friday rolls around, the team feels like it has been through the wringer and is ready for a break. Sunday evening, the drill begins again with a forwarded note from the head of strategy with an urgent request to explore "what if" scenarios about a potential acquisition. In short order, the Board wants a Plan A and Plan B. Yet again, plans and priorities are set aside and a new set of activities begun urgently. Pete and his team are frustrated, but they soldier on, because what else can they do?

You may witness workplace scenes like this regularly or be the recipient of fire drill emails just when you are settled into a well-deserved dinner out. These adrenaline-filled, repeat experiences are exhausting and even a bit demoralizing. And they are becoming way too common.

It's no secret that myriad challenges exist with teams today - relationship strains, dawn to dusk workplace cultures, lack of strategic alignment, plain old politics, and continued mergers and acquisitions that destabilize organizational structure. Underneath all of this, glimpses of rogue behavior and territory protection emerge and feelings of uncertainty, scarcity and self-preservation arise. You might be wondering if life in the corporate workplace is forever upended, but fear not, hope, skills, and trust still win the day.

But where do you begin?

Effective leadership, both individually and collectively, is highly correlated with positive business performance and greater levels of employee engagement. That's not breaking news, but have you recently – or ever – taken the time to examine your own leadership effectiveness? Or do you feel caught in the cycle of work chaos and shrug your shoulders about what to do? Or do you sometimes just want to bury your head in the sand? Or worse yet, want to walk out the door and never come back?

Leadership Hero Code focuses on prevention of, and recovery from, systemic challenges that disrupt business as usual (BAU) and impede your leadership success. The current BAU often equates to an ever-increasing workload in a more complex reporting and working environment. **High-performing leaders today deplete two precious commodities – energy and time – to deliver on constantly changing corporate initiatives, address unexpected fire drills, and negotiate the political landscape. Some may view this as heroics, but the pace and output levels aren't sustainable.**

The time is now for a new way of doing business as usual.

The writer Ernest Hemingway (yes, I can claim a distant relation) was considered a "man's man" and a strong personality, yet relatable. His work and his characters embody his own values and way of thinking — intense masculinity and confidence that harmoniously coexist with sensitivity. Based on this he created a set of principles known as the "Code Hero" which is commonly defined as "a man who lives correctly, following the ideals of honor, courage and endurance in a world that is sometimes chaotic, often stressful, and always painful."[1]

Chaotic, stressful, painful. Isn't that how we characterize the work world today? The traits of Hemingway's Code Hero were that of courageousness, confidence, reflection, grace under pressure, individualism, and self-discipline. He also would include stoicism, but that is not a behavior that ultimately leads to fulfillment. Contemplation of how I marry different skills within my own life for navigating the uneven terrain of today's workplaces made me realize that I identify with the ideals of living correctly and following certain ideals as well. Thus, with a nod to Ernest and a twist of the words, I have created a leadership model called the **Leadership Hero Code**.

When you think about a hero, you think of someone brave and courageous. One definition of heroics, from lexico.com, is "behavior or talk that is bold, especially unexpectedly so," but what does that mean for you in your day-in day-out challenges at work? Do you feel bold? Or more like bowled over and overwhelmed?

If you have tried "just riding it out," you know the ride becomes quite bumpy. A never-ending one as well. Some leaders cope by doubling-down (comply – work harder and longer), some disengage (protect – enter sarcasm and silos), while others become overly directive and autocratic (control – and perfection) in an effort to control the chaos. While these coping mechanisms can work in the short term, they have significant consequences on vitality and physical health as well as mental and emotional health. Your job starts to feel more like an endurance race just to garner a paycheck rather than a fulfilling career. I've worked alongside leaders as they've had their wake-up call and recognized they can no longer sustain such false heroics and are on the verge of personal crisis. At best, it is a crisis of the heart, and at its worst it can be a literal heart attack.

There is a different way.

Leadership Hero Code is essentially a new system of values. My desire in writing this book is to equip you to respond confidently and authentically as you navigate today's complex, ambiguous and often unpredictable workplace. You will discover how to recalibrate your leadership and quality of life – and be able to create change, even in the most conservative environments. Truth be told, I've even employed these principles out in nature, on challenging hikes where competing personalities and capabilities put the group at risk.

How can this be achieved? You need trustworthy diagnostics you can count on to help focus your attention on high-impact areas that increase or deter your effectiveness as a leader. That is exactly what we delve into here in these pages.

An abundance of courage is required to face and create change. Leadership Hero Code will support you as you journey forward to be your own kind of hero. Come be part of this change movement with me.

"THERE IS NOTHING NOBLE IN BEING SUPERIOR TO YOUR FELLOW MEN. TRUE NOBILITY LIES IN BEING SUPERIOR TO YOUR FORMER SELF."

ERNEST HEMINGWAY

CHAPTER 1:
THE DESIRE FOR MORE

Not everyone wants "more" in the traditional sense. In fact, many want "less" – fewer demands, fewer deadlines, fewer unanticipated stressors. The "more" I bring forward here is the recognition that our minutes, hours and days could be more meaningful and provide more energy and more optimism. This book is for you, and the teams you engage with, if you long for a better way to experience that kind of "more" in your day-to-day life.

Let's start where we spend one third (or more) of our time, at the workplace. Realistically, we are one "whole" person who experiences a personal life and a professional life, but let's face it, the content of our workday influences who we are in the evening, how we relate to family and friends, and even how we sleep and dream. What goes on at work does not just affect your professional life, it affects your whole life.

Feeling passionate and "of use" as a leader is imperative – and a critical rite of passage to owning your impact and shaping your world more fully. In today's difficult and stress-inducing workplace community, it can be easier to move toward self-absorption as a protective mechanism or way to insulate against the increasing white noise. The stress may seem enough to induce the fight, flight or freeze response. While the temptation to start sleep walking is great, don't! You might presently be feeling down and out, and it's understandable if optimism feels like a pipe dream. The fact is that work today is tough.

But you are tougher.

Now is the time to be courageous and explore what is possible. Now is the time to adhere to this new set of core principles, the Leadership Hero Code, which in essence serve as a guidepost to keep you on track for your own, and your team's, optimal performance.

In the coming chapters, you will complete some diagnostics in support of your leadership health. Think of these indicators as check-ups that provide insight on specific ways you can experiment with skills and see the impact immediately.

Let's take a quick look at some of the factors contributing to the stress, fatigue and overload in today's workplace so you can understand the playing field.

YOUR PERSONAL HEALTH STATUS IS LINKED TO YOUR WORKPLACE

There is a demonstrated link between an organization's culture and your personal health. We're not just talking about workplace safety in the traditional sense, but rather, the degree to which the cultural biome positively or negatively influences your well-being and leadership potency. Organizational cultures that don't support leadership growth statistically show diminished health status in their workforce.[2] Work-related stress is now the leading workplace health concern, even above physical inactivity and obesity. Therefore, it is absolutely critical that you take a step back and look at the impact of your environment on your overall well-being.

Seriously, take a pause and do so this very moment. Take a deep breath and think about your current work situation. What does your intuition tell you right now about the impact of your workplace on your overall health? And your effectiveness in your role?

YOUR CONFIDENCE AND MINDSET ARE INFLUENCED BY YOUR WORKPLACE

Your work environment affects how you think globally about your life and impacts your level of psychological well-being.[3] More specifically, the degree to which you are confident in your performance and are willing to raise risks and concerns is key, and of course much higher inside organizational cultures with strong managerial communication skills. What is the organizational culture that you enter every day?

In a recent study, a staggering sixty-two percent of employees agreed that their work culture made them feel less confident in their performance. Further, sixty-nine percent reported it was safer to remain silent about their workplace stress.[4] Feeling confident and able to speak up are critical parts of being effective and feeling good at work. Do an on-the-spot evaluation of your status right now. What is your current level of confidence – or stress – about your performance in your workplace?

YOUR LEADERSHIP WELL-BEING IS IMPACTED BY THE MEETING PROTOCOLS AT WORK

Meetings! It feels like that should be a four-letter word! We spend increasing amounts of time in scheduled or impromptu meetings solving for today's problems or planning for the future. This means that time is increasingly a commodity. In fact, meetings have increased in length and frequency over the past fifty years, to the point where executives spend an average of nearly 23 hours a week in meetings.[5] If there were such a thing as a 40-hour workweek, half the time being spent in meetings is draining and frustrating.

Also, this meeting schedule comes at the expense of deep-thinking time, which is crucial. As a consultant, I rely heavily upon deep-thinking time, uninterrupted windows where I can creatively problem solve and develop content. Too much time in meetings is counter-productive, to say the least. How are you affected by meetings? What is the pace of your meeting schedule, and what are the consequences of this pace?

YOUR RESTORATIVE SLEEP IS IMPACTED BY DYNAMICS IN YOUR WORKPLACE

Organizations with extreme pressure on project turnaround time or email response time place great demands on their employees which often results in compromised sleep and thus performance. A recent study reported that sixty-six percent feel that workplace issues negatively affect their sleep, and half of respondents engage in unhealthy behaviors to cope with workplace stress.[6] Many situations at work affect your mood and stay with you when you lie down in bed at night, even if you are not consciously dwelling on the issues.

The fact that there is stress or upheaval or nonstop commitments is a silent weight on your shoulders and that can affect the quality of your sleep. How well you sleep affects how well you function. Powering through with coffee or energy drinks is not a sustainable solution.

Ask yourself: What is the quality of my sleep in the peaks and valleys of my workplace environment?

YOUR SENSE OF STABILITY IS IMPACTED BY THE CHANGE ENVIRONMENT AT WORK

A central feature of many work environments is rapid change, organizational restructure and diminished "support" of individual development and day-to-day guidance. This type of environment often creates a survival mentality. Recent research shows that the average organization has undergone five enterprise changes in the past three years and seventy-three percent of organizations expect more change initiatives in the next few years.[7] In my experience with mergers and acquisitions, even one large change every eighteen months has a cascade effect on how clearly people understand their roles, chief priorities, and leadership structure.

Even though we all know that the only constant is change, being in the whirlwind that never seems to let up affects you whether you are a worrier or not. Reflect on your role currently or in the past year. How does the level of change in your work environment impact your confidence and ability to lead?

THERE IS HOPE

I share these factors not to dishearten you, but for you to check in and see if any of these themes are part of your regular work experience. Most organizations have pockets where some of these circumstances are heightened – a transition in leadership to an outside recruit, a failed digital transformation project, a performance improvement plan that is heading south. Answer honestly: Is your quality of life impacted by one or more of these factors on a regular basis? My guess is that your answer is yes.

That is where the Leadership Hero Code comes in. You are now well aware of the chips stacked against you, and you will discover how to topple them. You can create a new Business As Usual where you feel replenished and energized at the end of the day. Your personal life will not be spent "recovering" from your work life. Instead of binge-watching Netflix or eating junk food or any other habits we engage in just to muster up strength to face another workday, you will feel revitalized. But getting there takes courage.

What does courage in the workplace look like for you? Where does work feel like a #win with abundant energy and satisfaction? Just as important to recognize: Where does work feel like #hereweareagain and a drain on your energy? The more aware you become, the stronger leader you become.

FINDING AN ANTIDOTE TO STRESS

My client, Dante, a leader in a large health system, is responsible for managing digital clinical content that can often span thousands of pages. Physicians and hospital administrators often barrage him with requests that require quick turnaround, 100% accuracy, and an unfortunate level of order-taking. This environment causes Dante to operate with a measure of guardedness and masking. Dante confided to me one day that his antidote to the stress is writing fiction early in the morning before he leaves for work. As it turns out, he's published seven novels, all written between the hours of 3:30am – 6:30am on weekdays.

As he talked about his writing, Dante simply beamed with satisfaction and showed me his latest book cover. I had never seen him look this sprightly. I had him ponder what aspect of the workplace also made him feel this kind of alive. My first challenge to Dante was: How can you find more interest and openings for participation in the actual workday itself so that your life feels more integrated overall? At first, he laughed sarcastically, but then contemplated, "Well, I do think I could participate more in meetings where assignments are given out. Usually I wait and take what I am handed with resignation." My second challenge to Dante a few weeks later was to see if he'd be willing to experiment (with an open mind) with how he interacts with his team and other teammates throughout the day.

I sat across from him in a meeting soon after and gave him a nod at a moment that was perfect for him to interject and share his opinion as a contribution to the team conversation. He took the cue and spoke. People raised their eyebrows at first but then nodded in agreement. Dante walked out with a smile and acknowledged that engaging more was satisfying.

Dante is now able to show up more often as himself in his team meetings versus wearing the guarded mask of the past. Interestingly, he noted that as he now no longer goes underground and disengages at work, he is less prone to catching colds and taking sick days off. Dante is also more aware of how his behavior, attitude, and environment at work affects his overall well-being.

In what circumstances do you reserve or hold back your "true self" in a team environment? What do you typically hold back on? What do you more frequently decide to offer? Your answers to these questions should tie back to the five workplace stress factors you contemplated a few minutes ago.

This book is about taking on a grander experiment for your life, starting with where you put your feet every Monday through Friday. If you are courageous and unwilling to live in the status quo, you can take control over your work life and leadership effectiveness by experimenting with these targeted leadership principles. That is what the Leadership Hero Code is about – a set of "ground rules" to live by for that "more" in overall well-being, for your whole life. We use these indicators to show us where we need to focus or refocus. When you know where you're off the map you can continually course-correct to be the best and highest version of you.

You can no longer sacrifice the lion's share of your energy and time. It's time to reclaim your work well-being and sense of hope. Be among those who will speak up and contribute to creating and upholding quality work cultures that support leaders.

Use this book as a tool for active contemplation of your own leadership. Do the exercises. Work through the diagnostics and specific skills to conduct your own change experiments. At the end of each chapter, you are provided key take-aways and an inquiry – a homework assignment in wonder (read: fun, not algebra!). Let this book crack the code for you.

Here is a preview of the topics:

- **Three Principles for Personal Leadership Health:** You will step through an individual leadership well-being check. There are some easy exercises that help illuminate your state of mind and "being" as you lead at work or in a team. The specific areas we explore are Managing Your Energy Bank, Sense of Purpose, and Attention to Self-Care.

- **Four Principles for Team Leadership Health:** Building off your individual leadership health insights, you will examine the nature of your team's leadership ecosystem and culture. You will analyze four areas that help you create a snapshot of your team's current-state leadership effectiveness: Collective Energy, Psychological Safety, Authentic Exchanges, and Vital Conversations.

- **Linking Leadership Principles to Purpose:** Beyond these seven standards, this chapter is a cross-check for you regarding whether there is a clear "why" behind your team's existence.
A strategic framework is needed for creating clearer purpose as the backbone for a productive leadership culture.

- **Integrating Individual and Team Leadership Principles:** Test out a simple and practical leadership model to consider the skills and behaviors you want to model.

- **Moving Your Team into Action:** Begin to design experiments or "proof of concepts" to gauge impact with intention in your leadership choices.

- **Bonus Experiments:** Ideas and prompts to consider as you design your experiments - so you can move forward confidently.

If more confidence, more breathing room, and more mastery – a life where you can contribute more and get more in return – is the "more" you seek, let's begin!

> "DO YOU HAVE THE COURAGE TO SHOW UP FULLY IN YOUR LIFE, EVEN WHEN YOU ARE NOT SURE WHAT WILL HAPPEN?"
>
> BRENÉ BROWN

your own leadership development journey and recognize the opportunities you will have to choose ways of leading and living your life that are fulfilling.

In the next few chapters, we explore the two foundational health principles – Managing Your Energy, Attending to Your Purpose, and Attention to Self-Care – that we hope will offer you rich insights about your leadership and its impact on others.

> "DO YOU HAVE THE COURAGE TO SHOW UP FULLY IN YOUR LIFE, EVEN WHEN YOU ARE NOT SURE WHAT WILL HAPPEN?"
>
> — BRENÉ BROWN

CHAPTER 2:
THREE PRINCIPLES FOR PERSONAL LEADERSHIP HEALTH

Every year (hopefully), you schedule a visit with your primary care physician and get an annual well-being check. Many organizations require them in order to provide you with a subsidized insurance premium. Regardless, annual checks feature the usual vitals like blood pressure, weight, cholesterol and any changes in health or life status. These baselines help you and your doctor know what's "normal" given your history and what may be a new concern. A shift in these markers can cause us to look at underlying patterns or habits that have formed to explain why something is off or different.

This type of annual well-being check doesn't really exist in the workplace as it relates to your leadership "health." Of course, performance reviews are conducted annually using a standard form and scale in categories such as results-orientation, teamwork, innovation, profit and margins, etc. The missing factor is your own assessment of how effective, confident and energized you are in your role as a leader.

What I offer here is an individual leadership well-being check that starts with your own personal assessment. What does this mean? A leadership well-being check is a way for you to honestly examine yourself using indicators that gauge the degree to which you are engaged, living and leading thoughtfully, and satisfied with your overall quality of life when you are operating in a team environment.

Why is this important? There is a proven, statistical correlation between personal leadership effectiveness and business performance.[8] Vice versa, the degree to which you are engaged in your own leadership development and growth, the more opportunities you will have to choose work environments and careers that are fulfilling. This is a two-way street!

In the next few chapters, we explore three specific leadership health principles – Managing Your Energy Bank, Sense of Purpose, and Attention to Self-Care – that if carefully observed, offer you rich insights about your leadership and ability to impact on others.

> "KNOWING YOURSELF IS THE BEGINNING OF ALL WISDOM."
>
> — ARISTOTLE

CHAPTER 3:
PERSONAL LEADERSHIP HEALTH PRINCIPLE #1: YOUR ENERGY BANK

Think about a more complex project you are working on right now. This could be volunteer work, an entrepreneurial endeavor, or life inside a corporation. In general, what does your energy bank feel like when you are regularly in this environment?

Let's define energy bank as the gas tank you bring to that project or workplace environment and what it looks like when you leave that environment. Are you often running on empty or does your environment actually replenish you on the whole?

In this chapter we explore the tangible and intangible factors that impact your energy bank, and we begin to design some experiments to see what can improve or shift. This may sound like a "soft" indicator, but in reality, it's foundational. The ability to manage your energy bank and adjust the dial and take timely steps to preserve energy dictates the longevity and productivity of your leadership.

WHEN WORK IS YOUR LIFE

Elijah, a former colleague, was a 41-year-old management consultant, married with a two-year old daughter and a baby on the way. He wanted to balance the load of family responsibilities with his wife, Alexis, but Elijah was on the partner track. There were great demands on his time for new business development, project delivery, and periodic assignments to test his fitness for moving to partner. What was once limited travel and the occasional long day became one to two nights away each week plus several 15-hour days with teams onsite when he was not traveling. Elijah didn't feel like he could say no while being tested out as a partner. Caffeine and energy drinks became his "coping" mechanisms.

Elijah confided in me about this crunch time in his career and that he felt backed into a corner.

My question to him was simple: "What do you value most in your life right now?"

He said, "Taking care of my family through providing."

A few more months went by and the pace was relentless. Soon Elijah couldn't remember when he last exercised or had a Saturday free to be with his family. Fast forward and his daughters were now three years old and almost six months old. I was in a "war room" with him one night around 10pm working on a big presentation for the next day. I noticed he had a sheen on his face and was breathing heavily. Before I knew it, he clutched his heart and fainted on the table. I called 911. Elijah was taken to the hospital.

This was the case of a near miss...not a fatal heart attack, but heart disease coupled with severe stress and fatigue. Elijah, his wife and his physician decided a new path was needed or Elijah's health would continue to decline. He began working with a nutritionist and selected a new partner mentor to support him. In the first six weeks of this new experiment, Elijah's energy returned and his perspective on his priorities (personal health, family) enabled him to set boundaries and expectations more clearly at work. These were very courageous steps for a high-performing leader like Elijah to take.

No one wants or expects a heart attack, and perhaps it can be avoided by paying attention to your energy bank. Let's begin by taking a moment to identify some of the basic patterns you might have in an average workday.

In the table on the next page, think back to a recent day at work and make note of your energy level, feelings, and 'coping' mechanisms at five critical points in the day. Most likely, you will see how your energy ebbs and flows. In addition, you may see some emerging patterns around how you respond in these dips and peaks.

TIME OF DAY	OVERALL ENERGY LEVEL High, Medium, Low	"GENERAL FEELINGS" e.g., wiry, anxious	COPING MECHANISMS e.g., coffee, music
On way to work			
Arriving at work			
Lunch time			
Late afternoon			
Arriving home			

Let's drill a bit deeper. Specifically, what activities give you energy versus take or deplete your energy? Certainly, there are more mundane areas of our jobs that require some patience, so think about the "extremes" just to get a sense. If you are not in a corporate environment every day, perhaps you can look at a team you interact with regularly (sports, volunteer, church). Take a quick inventory on the worksheet below with a project in mind:

TAKE ENERGY (activities or interactions)	IMPACT ON ME	GIVE ENERGY (activities or interactions)	IMPACT ON ME
1.		1.	
2.		2.	
3.		3.	
4.		4.	
5.		5.	

Are there patterns in when and how you experience uplifting energy moments? What about the depleting ones? Keep these in mind as you read the story below.

YOUR ENERGY BANK IS GOLD

One of the most talented energy bank leaders I've worked with, Jana, is a partner with a global management consulting firm. She travels every week and has standardly long days. She is naturally jazzed about client business issues and gets energy from puzzling through their data, their concerns and potential solutions to meet their needs. Jana was in the process of building a new practice area and fell into a pattern traveling five days a week to create awareness of this offering nationally. Even with her love for her career, her energy bank was leaking during this time period.

Jana scheduled time with me, and we assessed her ability to manage her energy bank. Using the worksheet I created, we looked at times of day, circumstances and her overall energy bank changes throughout the course of a week. From there, we identified that her nutrition and exercise were being compromised. And, there were no breaks in her day anymore. Jana took a hard look at her diet and decided she felt better when she ate vegan (!). In addition, her back had been troubling her, so she decided to see a PT and begin some core strength exercises again. She also had her admin schedule two 20-minute breaks a day. Two months later, Jana had a lot more pep in her step. In fact, she said the adjustments overall boosted her daily energy bank by 30% (she is that precise).

Managing your energy bank is not a complex issue, but it needs to be honored. You face many challenges in today's multitasking, over-scheduled workplace. Paying attention to your energy bank can be the secret weapon in your arsenal as long as you can pivot quickly to fill your cup instead of depleting it. Personally, when I am exercising regularly and minding my energy bank at work, I have greater capacity to be in a high intensity work environment. I have an accountability partner I check in with from time to time, to get a reflection of how well I am leading with energy bank in mind. Consider having an "energy bank buddy" to keep you mindful of where you are spending your most precious resource. (And FYI, Elijah did make partner and continually keeps his eyes on his energy bank.)

KEY TAKE-AWAYS:

- You add to or deplete from your energy bank on a daily basis. An accumulation of depleting activities does impact outlook and overall leadership effectiveness.

- Your energy bank is influenced by a variety of factors, including nutrition, sleep, meeting pace, team culture and demands or stressors in workplace. Knowing which factors impact you most is the first step.

- You can influence your energy bank at work based on your explicit choices at moments throughout each day.

- You will be more successful if you have an accountability partner, and you support each other in low and high energy bank moments.

What are you learning about your own energy bank? The most important part is noticing how you are impacted by the environment around you and your choices in the moment during a workday.

To help you better be able to do this in the moment, write down two things you believe might help you protect and build your energy bank during the day at work.

1. _____

2. _____

> "TRUST IS SINGLE-HANDEDLY THE MOST POWERFUL SOURCE OF POSITIVE ENERGY AND, ONCE IN PLACE, UNLOCKS A FREEDOM AND PEACE TO EXPLORE."
>
> — ANGELA AHRENDTS

CHAPTER 4:
PERSONAL LEADERSHIP HEALTH PRINCIPLE #2: SENSE OF PURPOSE

The second element of your leadership health at work is sense of purpose. Another way of saying this: how clear are you about the mission of your organization and your expected contributions and rewards? The level of clarity contributes to, or diminishes, your confidence and overall well-being at work. Meaningful sense of purpose and direction not only increase your energy levels but also allow you to screen time and effort because you know how well a project or activity contributes to the bigger goal.

Based on a team role you hold today, take a moment and work through an initial worksheet on purpose-related indicators:

YOUR ROLE TODAY	LEVEL OF CLARITY	WHAT WOULD MAKE IT CLEARER?
My top three priorities	High/Medium/Low	
1.		
2.		
3.		

WHY I WAS HIRED/SELECTED		
1.		
2.		
3.		

WHAT I BELIEVE I EXCEL IN		
1.		
2.		
3.		

PURPOSE OF THE TEAM		
1.		
2.		
3.		
MY METRICS FOR SUCCESS		
1.		
2.		
3.		
DIRECTION FROM MY MANAGER		
1.		
2.		
3.		

What does this information tell you about your leadership role and what is expected of you? How clear is communication and guidance from your manager? As Bob Anderson and Bill Adams state in Mastering Leadership, "Leaders succeed or fail depending on whether or not they clarify role expectations and keep their promises."[8]

Embracing the Leadership Hero Code means that you take the necessary steps to get clear on your role expectations, and when dealing with your team, you communicate the reason for all objectives every step of the way. As you begin to understand how crucial sense of purpose is to your own well-being, you will begin to more readily accommodate that need in others as well.

CLARITY AND CONFIDENCE

Katelyn was known as a utility player within the Marketing department, able to take on various projects and help move them forward fairly independently. Then the organization began to grow rapidly over a five-year period through mergers and acquisitions. In the span of these years, Katelyn experienced three different department leaders and reported to four different managers. Her portfolio of work was changed up fairly regularly.

When her role was switched up again and she was asked to take on budget management and reporting for the department, I was brought in to help support her in this transition. One thing I knew - this new position was completely out of her wheelhouse. Her other two responsibilities were vastly different altogether. Katelyn began to feel like she got the leftovers and was taking on the projects that no one else wanted. Plus, she really wasn't comfortable in Excel and kept transposing numbers and formulas. Katelyn began losing confidence in her abilities and started feeling more disconnected from the broader department. Unfortunately, she sat in silence over this struggle. And at what cost?

In a karmic twist of events, Katelyn broke her foot stepping off a curb, had surgery and some post-op complications meant she had to take a few weeks off work to recover. I was asked to provide some interim support on budget management and reporting. What I discovered was that some of the tools and reports had incorrect formulas and totals, which could cause confusion in understanding remaining funds for the department. Katelyn returned to work and we sat side by side to review the modifications and create some check points where she could more easily confirm accuracy of numbers. During one of these side by side conversations, she said "I don't really understand my current role. Or why I was asked to lead budget. It really isn't comfortable for me no matter how hard I try, but I don't think I can bring this up to my manager. I don't think I have a choice anyway in what I do."

Leaders must have a clear sense of purpose or they can lose their footing. Further, if mission at hand does not align with the inherent or teachable skill sets, then you have double the trouble. I worked with Katelyn to outline some approaches she could take with her manager to begin the dialogue about her strengths, and to ask for exactly what she needed to be successful in leading the budget forward. She took the leap, had the conversation, and her manager agreed to see what they could do together. Ultimately, Katelyn acknowledged that quantitative detail work was not an

> inherent strength of hers and that she would be best suited to project management work and strategic initiatives. While this posed the short-term problem of finding a new budget lead, it caused great relief for both Katelyn and her manager. Clarity in her strengths and sense of purpose in her position were restored.

How high do the stakes need to be for you to ask for a clearer sense of mission – or ask for help because you feel your skills are not suited to an expected part of your job?

Purpose provides the ultimate direction for energy and decision making on a day-to-day basis. Remember that there is a difference between tasks we are asked to do that are routine or mundane and those that are beyond our natural aptitude. Holding informal check-ins with your boss can be done as part of a regular progress update. Ideally, you and your manager are aligned on key priorities and expectations – and the assignments align to your sense of purpose and skill in the workplace.

A good way to approach this foundational conversation is to cross-check team priorities, and make sure expectations of your role are clear. To prepare, you can think through the questions below and tailor them to give you maximum clarity on your purpose while also allowing room to acknowledge what you enjoy working on.

SAMPLE QUESTIONS/SCRIPT FOR YOU TO COURAGEOUSLY ADAPT FOR YOUR OWN CHECK-IN:

- Let's check in on our top priorities over the next few months. I think they are: (A) _____
  (B) _____ (C) _____

  - Does this align with your expectations?

- I see my role in these top priorities as: _____ .

  - Of these priorities, I generally find that _____

is (a better fit, easier, more exciting) for me and makes me feel like I am contributing in a meaningful way. Do you see this too?

- I wish I had more time to focus on _____ .

- _____ is a barrier for me, and is frustrating.

- I've tried_____, but would value your ideas and coaching.

- What do you want more of from me? _____

- What do you want less of from me? _____

KEY TAKE-AWAYS:

- You know you are operating on purpose if your energy bank feels generally full and you operate in the "flow" space, often losing track of time.

- On the flip side, you know if you are not operating in the zone of purpose you feel restless, anxious about performing and wonder about what project or role might be a better fit.

- Either way, having a discussion with your boss about your role, your purpose and aptitude in the role assigned to you is critical. You can begin with a singular project to ensure you are aligned if looking at your overall role seems overwhelming.

- What are you learning about your sense of purpose? The most important part is being aware of your charter and how your aptitude (skills) and desire (preference) meet around particular projects.

Write down two things you believe would help you operate from a sense of purpose and courage on a daily basis:

1. _____

2. _____

> "SUCCESS AS A LEADERSHIP TEAM IS TIED DIRECTLY TO OUR LEVEL OF ALIGNMENT ON VISION AND DIRECTION, OUR AGREEMENT ON KEY STRATEGIES, AND HOW WELL WE EXECUTE TOGETHER."
>
> BOB ANDERSON & BILL ADAMS

CHAPTER 5:
PERSONAL LEADERSHIP HEALTH PRINCIPLE #3: ATTENTION TO SELF-CARE

Self-care, by definition, is making choices to support sound physical, mental or spiritual well-being. Many lifestyle experts tout the merits of self-care for busy parents, but rarely is self-care discussed in the context of the workplace. Self-care has the power to transform your outlook and contributions both at home and at work.

What does self-care look like in general? It is as simple as time spent doing something that boosts your energy bank or your spirits. This is not an every-once-in-a-while effort, but should be proportionate to the amount of stress and strain you have in your work life.

Examples of self-care include:

- Attending a live sporting event or live music
- Playing with a pet
- Fixing something or building something
- Taking a walk outside
- Getting a vigorous workout in
- Regular massage or pedicures
- Getting your car detailed
- Having a special dinner out with a loved one
- Scheduling 30 minutes to do "nothing"

A PERENNIAL STRIVER MEETS BOUNDARIES

Laine is a regional marketing leader for a large healthcare system. She puts 100% effort into her role, her people, and the quality of her work. She strives to understand the strategic direction and rationale for certain decisions. As the organization grew through mergers and acquisitions, she experienced three new leaders within an 18-to-24-month period. Each one had a different interpretation of the direction her role should take. Each one had different understandings of healthcare operations, the needs of patients and "how" materials get produced in marketing. With every change, Laine asked clarifying questions, trying desperately to understand the landscape. Her energy levels dipped as she experienced "change fatigue."

Her workouts dwindled and her home life felt less connected. Through coaching and some much-needed vacation time, Laine shifted her strategy, and added back regular workouts to her schedule and one special outing a week with her husband as well as a daily 10-minute meditation break during the day. She also began to focus on the growth and development of her people. In addition, Laine began to take more ownership of her role – driving and clarifying an agenda for the geography in which she was located and working with clients. Not that she set aside the broader organizational purpose, but she took care of herself first – and redefined her more immediate sense of purpose in order to retain energy and feel more grounded.

Laine's story underscores that it is your responsibility as a leader to take stock at different points in the journey and make adjustments to your patterns. Self-care is definitely in the eye of the beholder, but must be implemented by all.

For me, I know that moments in nature help me re-set my perspective. In my personal life, I plan two big hiking trips a year to ensure a broader vista and break from every day routine. At work, I have a favorite park near my office that I glance at during conference calls or walk to regularly.

Take a moment now to think about the activities that might feel like self-care to you.

PERSONAL LIFE

ACTIVITIES I CONSIDER SELF-CARE	FREQUENCY (TODAY)	DESCRIBE HOW YOU FEEL WHEN YOU COMPLETE THIS ACTIVITY?
Example: get together with friends to watch a game	1x month	Connected, relaxed

WORK LIFE

ACTIVITIES I CONSIDER SELF-CARE	FREQUENCY (TODAY)	DESCRIBE HOW YOU FEEL WHEN YOU COMPLETE THIS ACTIVITY?
Example: schedule lunch out with a colleague	1x month	Part of something bigger, motivated to keep trying

What are you discovering from these exercises? Are there places you give yourself permission for self-care? Do you feel guilty taking time for yourself?

We need to normalize self-care so that you don't look at it as indulgence. The topic of self-care is fairly prevalent, even if the practice isn't, among women. However, for men, this has often been neglected as a topic or seen as more female-oriented.

In a recent study, more than 1,000 men nationally over the age of eighteen were interviewed around perceptions of self-care and perceived barriers to self-care. Almost sixty percent of the men who were surveyed acknowledged participating in more self-care practices over the past five years.[9] Increased energy and clearer thinking were some of the primary benefits reported.

Notable business leaders who embrace self-care find it fuels them with more creativity and innovation. In fact, during his early White House days, Barack Obama had a standing date in the evenings – not to sift through paperwork or make business calls, but to play pool with a friend. In addition, he made a commitment to have dinner with Michelle and the girls every night.

Kristen Neff, prominent researcher and thought leader, says "I found in my research that the biggest reason people aren't more self-compassionate is that they are afraid they'll become self-indulgent. They believe self-criticism is what keeps them in line. Most people have gotten it wrong because our culture says being hard on yourself is the way to be."[10] Being a powerful leader means taking an interest in your physical and mental health.

New entrants to self-care include millennial women who, according to a recent survey, are moving away from solely physical and financial goals to make self-care and mental health their priority.[11] Men and women of all ages need to follow suit.

Beyond academic and scientific support of the concept of self-care, intuitively you probably recognize that what works for one colleague (e.g. going to see one live music event a week) doesn't feel like self-care to another. You do what serves you. Self-care is an act of courage and is ultimately one of the most rewarding things you can do to support your leadership.

KEY TAKE-AWAYS:

- Self-care can make all the difference at work, regardless of your level, gender or circumstance.

- Scheduling your day based on self-care intentions and needs will inevitably add to your energy bank and outlook – even if what is planned gets interrupted sometimes.

- You might be surprised at the conversations you have with peers about how they integrate self-care into their day. Try it!

What are you learning about the role of self-care in your life? The most important part is noticing the moments that reset or restore you during the day.

Write down two self-care steps you could incorporate into your workday:

1. _____

2. _____

"GOOD SELF-CARE IS TYPICALLY MORE DIFFICULT AND LESS GLAMOROUS THAN TREATING YOURSELF… IT MEANS DOING THINGS LIKE HAVING GOOD SLEEP HYGIENE, GETTING A LITTLE MORE EXERCISE, STAYING HYDRATED, TAKING MEDICATION AS PRESCRIBED, EATING AT REGULAR INTERVALS, CREATING HEALTHY BOUNDARIES AND TAKING A BREAK FROM SOCIAL MEDIA."

EMILY BILEK

CHAPTER 6:
FOUR PRINCIPLES FOR TEAM LEADERSHIP HEALTH

The Leadership Hero Code maxims of managing your energy bank, sense of purpose, and attention to self-care are the foundation of your personal leadership health. Taking care of you must come first. Think of the often-used analogy that in case of emergency on a plane, you must put on your oxygen mask first before being able to assist another. The same logic applies to your leadership capabilities. You work on you then you are able to turn your attention to your team.

So, let's now look at the team ecosystem and four specific principles behind team leadership health. These precepts relate directly to your personal leadership health, and also serve to identify how you impact the system and where you can contribute more and get more in return. Remember that the ultimate goal is less stress and more fulfillment.

Regardless of whether you are an individual contributor, run an independent business from home, volunteer at a church, or fly to client sites every week, you are part of a team in some way. How you show up as a leader and how you interact with others – including individuals, teams, and organizations - impacts the entire ecosystem.

Take a moment to think about a team or group of people that you are working with now on a specific objective. What does this team environment look and feel like? Get out your pen or pencil and actually jot down your answers to the following:

TEAM MEMBERS: _____

GOALS: _____

- Who is the "customer" or end user of your team's outputs?
- What role do you play on this team?
- What are three things that are working well?
- What specifically is challenging?

The team leadership well-being check includes four criteria that reveal how aligned and engaged your team is collectively, and where you have opportunity to impact the ecosystem. This is about "what" the team does and also about "how" the team does it.

Below is a high-level view of these four indicators.

- **Collective Energy:** the intangible but clear tone and mood of an intact team; this energy often mirrors the values of the leader or a dominant team member.

- **Psychological Safety:** the degree to which team members feel confident in their performance and are willing to speak up about risks and concerns.

- **Authentic Exchanges:** the genuine and healthy regard team members extend to each other as they meet, pass in the hall or reference each other.

- **Vital Conversations:** the degree to which the real issues are addressed using straight talk rather than talking around or being politically correct.

There is much that is said, and unsaid, in any organization and that ongoing dynamic influences productivity, alignment and career satisfaction. To up your game as a leader, honest evaluation of how you enrich these following four areas can improve your leadership effectiveness and your entire life.

"PEOPLE NEED TO KNOW THAT THEY HAVE ALL THE TOOLS WITHIN THEMSELVES. SELF-AWARENESS, WHICH MEANS AWARENESS OF THEIR BODY, AWARENESS OF THEIR MENTAL SPACE, AWARENESS OF THEIR RELATIONSHIPS - NOT ONLY WITH EACH OTHER, BUT WITH LIFE AND THE ECOSYSTEM."

DEEPAK CHOPRA

CHAPTER 7:
TEAM LEADERSHIP HEALTH PRINCIPLE #1: COLLECTIVE ENERGY

You have now spent time in the personal leadership chapters raising awareness of how your work environment impacts you and how you respond in more fulfilling ways. Addressing your individual well-being in the workplace is the critical precursor to how you show up as a leader and how your own leadership shift can be an impetus for change within the team. Now you are ready to take a "gut check" on the energy of the team. The collective energy of a team can be sensed in a number of ways – attitude, sentiment or the general "undercurrent" of mood within the team. One giveaway moment is usually at the opening of a meeting when the leader introduces the agenda and the team begins to dialogue. The initial tone of the meeting, whether it feels upbeat or chaotic or lethargic, immediately shapes the quality of thinking and engagement from team members.

You probably thought of an example immediately of how the collective energy feels within your team. Take a moment to think about a specific recent challenging meeting with your team or a subgroup within your team and gauge the mood. Was there a feeling of excitement? Of deflation?

The purpose of the meeting was:_____
_____.

We tried to determine: _____
_____.

But we had these challenges:_____
_____.

To summarize this meeting, two words come to mind: _____ and _____ .

Now let's go one level deeper on a team meeting scenario. Below is an easy checklist you can apply to begin to notice the collective energy of the group. Awareness is the first step, then determining how and when to shift the collective energy is second.

MEETING EXAMPLE: _____

TOUCHPOINTS IN A MEETING	ENERGY INDICATORS (CHECK FOR POSITIVE, X FOR NEGATIVE)	SPECIFICALLY, I NOTICE (ATTITUDE, ATMOSPHERE, EMOTIONS)
Opening or Agenda Setting	• *Verbal cues* • *Body language* • *Clarity of agenda* • *Active listening*	
Decision-Making During Meeting	• *Sense of excitement* • *Level of inclusiveness* • *Exploration of choices*	
Closing of the Meeting	• *Level of satisfaction with discussion* • *Clarity on next steps* • *Sense of closure*	
Post-Meeting "Walkout" Feeling	• *Sense of progress* • *Clear assignments* • *Am I clear why I was here?*	

As I look back on these notes, I would say the collective energy of the team in this setting was: _____
_____ .

High-performing teams exhibit patterns in their energy indicators that propel momentum, inform decision making, and fuel optimism and productivity. These patterns typically include constructive language rather than skepticism, shared voices rather than one dominant voice, and building off others' ideas with something like a "yes, and" instead of a "no, but." When there is skepticism, domination and shooting down of ideas, there is a weight to the collective energy that hampers participation. Specific tools or tactics you can deploy include:

- Reframing – you can respond to sarcasm or skepticism by using language like "let's look at this from a few different perspectives…" and back it up with two examples or ideas.

- Spreading participation – you can step in and say "I'd like to hear from others around the table as well" and ask one or two specific people to comment in addition to the dominant player.

- Building from yes – if ideas are taking a left-hand turn, you can say "what I like about that is…" and then say "and, I want to add a related thought."

Now zoom out to the team you work with most often in a group setting. Here you will look at both the doing or activity-driven energy and the being or the climate energy.

DOING: How does the collective energy of the team show up around the "doing" activities (executing projects, analyzing results)?

BEING: How does the collective energy of the team show up relative to the "being" (attitude, climate, conflict)?

Notice whether one dimension impacts your quality of life at work more than the other.

Did you notice patterns?

SHAPING COLLECTIVE ENERGY THROUGH MENTORING

Theo made partner at an early age at the boutique consulting firm where he'd worked for the last fourteen years. His win rate on proposals was extraordinarily high, and he was always a client favorite in quality assurance reviews, yet his demeanor remained humble. As the firm and Theo's career continued to grow, he and I discussed his stellar achievements and what was next on the horizon for him as he had already achieved so much. We talked about his own individual well-being indicators and his deep sense of purpose. Even though he was still young and had plenty of career ahead of him, Theo felt called to be a "legacy" impactor.

He began writing books that garnered positive attention with clients and prospective clients. Forbes asked him to become a regular columnist on the topic of brand and growth. Theo enjoyed this facet of his skill sharing and wanted to do more. He got excited as he talked about a project in which he was mentoring a junior partner. Together, we looked at what his legacy could be if he was giving back and mentoring individuals and teams to work together with passion and dedication. As Theo moved forward, he injected every interaction with sincere enthusiasm and interest. He leveraged his own leadership success to bring others into the fold and create a collective energy that was greater than the sum of the parts. Among other things, his legacy included co-authoring another book with an up and coming colleague, helping to onboard a new partner to the firm, and creating an annual non-profit volunteer day for the firm. People at all levels in the firm were inspired to look on the bright side of long consulting hours and contribute to a positive culture and collective energy.

Setting the tone for the collective energy can happen from many different chairs, not just the CEO's, and creates a lasting ripple effect.

Reflect back on your personal leadership health diagnostics. How much of your well-being is influenced by the team energy you walk into every day? My guess is at least fifty percent! Flip this thinking, and how do you think your own personal energy contributes to the team environment? Exactly. You are responsible for how you show up, and now you are seeing more clearly how your attitude and behavior impacts those around you. Becoming your own leadership hero means being accountable for your personal contributions to the team ecosystem.

Beyond sensing the environment, the most important opportunity is choosing to take a timely action to contribute to the agenda and shape the energetic narrative of the meeting – on a regular basis. One interjection or observation can perhaps temporarily adjust the climate control, while regular participation begins to change neural pathways for a team. In this way, you will naturally recruit allies who see you modeling positive behaviors and feel compelled to contribute alongside.

The Leadership Hero Code is a proactive model. You are co-creating in any situation and we are all responsible. Individual effectiveness and team effectiveness go hand in hand. Being this kind of hero means opening up to possibilities and being a leader no matter your role. You can lead from the front of the room, the back of the room, the side of the room. Applying the tools and techniques provided here can make a difference, sometimes immediately and always over time. The first step is to understand that your behavior matters. Taking ownership of your attitude and actions is empowering. As a high performing leader, you realize that awareness is part of your skill set and focusing that awareness in the right areas can have tremendous and lasting impact.

KEY TAKE-AWAYS:

- Learning to read the collective energy of a team is a practical and tangible skill set.

- Once you master awareness and interpretation of collective energy, you can begin to use your leadership strengths to influence the environment.

- Influencing the environment is not an intermittent activity, but a way to show up as a leader and shape the narrative and energy while engaging others as allies.

- What are you learning about collective energy?

Write down an opportunity you have this week to notice the collective energy and how you can be a greater and more positive influence: _____

_____

_____

_____

_____.

"THE KEY TAKEAWAY IS THAT EFFECTIVE LEADERSHIP TRANSFORMS PEOPLE EMOTIONALLY, BUT ALSO COGNITIVELY. IN THE ENVIRONMENT ENERGIZED BY THE RIGHT LEADERSHIP, WE TAP INTO HIDDEN STRENGTHS AND BECOME BETTER VERSIONS OF OURSELVES: SEEING MORE, DOING MORE, LEARNING MORE."

BRETT STEENBARGER

CHAPTER 8:
TEAM LEADERSHIP HEALTH PRINCIPLE #2: PSYCHOLOGICAL SAFETY

The collective energy of a team serves as the backdrop for the other tenets of the Leadership Hero Code regarding team health and your leadership effectiveness. In regard to psychological safety, collective energy contributes to, or detracts from, the ability of team members to speak their mind and bring forward risks without fear of repercussion.

A mentor of mine used to say that safety is an inside job. This statement puzzled me, but then I realized that how well each of us knows our inner terrain and trusts our own ability to navigate the world and workplace affects how we show up as leaders. By becoming the best and highest version of ourselves, we can ensure a degree of stability and imperviousness in unpredictable times.

As individual leaders, we can master our own sense of safety and grounding. And, even so, there are times when unforeseen circumstances or unexpected behaviors can upset the balance of feeling safe in your team setting.

Think about a situation where you were with a team and one or two individuals tilted the atmosphere towards feeling too dangerous to show up open or to be candid. A recent study shows that more than two-thirds of people in the workplace prefer to stay silent about a risk or concern for fear of retaliation.[12] I am 100% sure you've encountered this at some point in your career or personal life.

When safety is present, rich ideas, solutions and energy flow and move freely. When safety is not present, a constriction occurs and you tend to see withholding, withdrawing or protecting behaviors in either glimpses or tidal waves. A lack of safety squashes your energy bank and stifles new ideas and creativity. Ultimately, this impacts not only team efficacy, but also business results.

Main components of a culture of safety in the workplace include:

- Information transparency exists
- Raising business and personnel risks is both relevant and welcome
- Eye contact and focused attention is a regular part of 1:1 interaction
- There is reciprocity of idea sharing, not simply an "order-taking" exercise for one side of the table
- There is no fear of retribution or retaliation for an opposing viewpoint

When some of these factors are missing, psychological safety is affected. Certainly, you can think of instances in your team culture where you have experienced less than ideal safety situations.

> **A BULLY IN THE BOARD ROOM**
>
> Gary was experienced and could have been a strong asset to the team, but in reality, he was a bully. If it's true that attitude is everything, then Gary was everything no one wanted to work with. It's a shame actually. He was intelligent but used his fast-thinking and rapid-fire commentary to create doubt within the team and cloud decision making. He excelled in creating unsafe environments where people didn't engage in dialogue authentically. In a team meeting one day, he used his large physical size to block a team member, Kimberly, from being able to exit the room. His antics resembled a boy in junior high, but this was not a playground. He simply laughed, but his behavior made everyone uncomfortable.

A few weeks after her run in, Kimberly talked with a colleague who had a long track record of interacting with Gary. A little more sleuthing, and it was clear that several people had their own negative experiences with Gary. Kimberly took summary concerns to an HR business partner. Managers and up on the team were asked if they had any negative experiences with Gary, and six out of ten came forward to share verbal altercations or stonewalling stories. Gary was assigned a workplace mentor and an executive coach. After six months of coaching and being monitored, Gary decided to relocate to another state and take an executive role where he could run the show. Hopefully his leadership and collaboration skills have improved. No one from his previous department regretted providing facts and stories about the impact of an unsafe psychological environment. A few weeks after Gary left, members of the team remarked how much more productive and at ease they were. The psychological safety was restored and the collective energy re-energized.

Let's work through a specific scenario in your world. Take inventory of one team setting you inhabit today where you have a hunch some element of safety is being compromised, and work through these steps.

Identify a moment when you did not feel comfortable bringing forward a question or concern.

- What was the energy in that moment? Can you describe it using a metaphor?

- Think about the person that was compromising the safety; how would you describe the impact?

- What do you think their motivation was?

- What might be a "brave" action you could take that would feel both authentic and safe in this team environment?

Being a leadership hero includes being brave to change a situation. Brave actions are many and can look like the following:

- Naming what is happening in the space (John, it feels like you are blocking this project, what is going on?)

- Scheduling a meeting to include advocates for the project, so that you are not alone with a "bully" or adversarial team member.

- Asking for a stand-in (Gary, it seems like you are distracted, is there a stand-in you would like to nominate for this meeting?)

Often a brave action is simply voicing your concerns. I bring up safety and bullying for a reason, because these elements usually do not co-exist. You cannot truly win with a bully or an energy vampire, but you can convert advocates of constructive conversations and even those "on the edge." The more you evaluate and focus on your own leadership health, the more you will see your effectiveness increase. Psychological safety can grow, even in teams where it seems fragile. When you feel stronger from an individual well-being perspective, you are able to see and address the issue of safety within the team.

As you are well aware, the consequences of an unsafe environment are significant. Not only does this atmosphere undermine productivity and sense of mission but it also elicits reactions that can be quite divisive. At the other end of the spectrum, a safe environment naturally encourages the flow of ideas, creative problem solving and rising momentum. A healthy and safe environment also allows more space and trust for humor, camaraderie and engagement.

BUILDING A HIGH RELIABILITY CULTURE

Avery, a healthcare executive, spent years studying other categories and industries and how they reduce preventable acts of harm. She found the airline industry, armed forces and manufacturing companies have long believed in creating cultures of high-reliability or safety. This means having an environment that listens to and welcomes questions and concerns that could impact the customer or employee. Avery developed the business case for introducing high reliability practices into the hospital she led, and funding was approved. Over a period of three years, she worked with consultants and staff, both clinical and non-clinical, to embed behaviors and practices that encourage risk identification with no punitive after-effects – in fact, positive after-effects. I supported Avery in the development of training materials and the internal roadshow to garner leadership support. This was a multi-year journey, and the preventable acts of harm decreased by almost seventy-five percent in the first three years. In addition, employee engagement surveys demonstrated a more engaged and confident workforce. This is a stunning example of creating psychological safety, for the sake of patients and employees, and is doable in any industry or work climate.

Avery and Gary couldn't be more different. I am sure you have witnessed these extremes as well. The goal is to actively cultivate safety across all levels in the team.

KEY TAKE-AWAYS:

- A psychologically safe workplace is critical for innovation and growth, as well as raising risks and concerns that impact employees and customers.

- When there is a bully or someone who disrupts the space, it can be terribly frustrating for the team and often impacts a wide circle of people, not just the target.

- Safe workplaces are built over time, and with consistent leadership and participation. You can contribute to this space by taking one brave action at a time (e.g. stating your opinion, naming a behavior that is not acceptable).

What are you learning about your psychological safety at work? The most important part is noticing how the environment shifts when one individual makes it either safe or unsafe for others to speak up or have an opposing viewpoint.

Write down a brave action you might take if someone compromised psychological safety for you or a trusted team member:

_____

_____

_____

_____

_____ .

"IF LEADERS WANT TO UNLEASH INDIVIDUAL AND COLLECTIVE TALENT, THEY MUST FOSTER A PSYCHOLOGICALLY SAFE CLIMATE WHERE EMPLOYEES FEEL FREE TO CONTRIBUTE IDEAS, SHARE INFORMATION, AND REPORT MISTAKES."

— AMY C. EDMONDSON

CHAPTER 9:
TEAM LEADERSHIP HEALTH PRINCIPLE #3: AUTHENTIC EXCHANGES

In this chapter we look closely at positive team interactions and how, over time, they help create shared understanding and increased participation. Let's define an authentic exchange as an earnest conversation between two individuals where trust deposits occur because the two people are "real" with each other. Where do you experience this in your daily dealings with colleagues? Is trust guarded? Do people hesitate to be genuine?

THE GLOSSY COVER

Regina was newly elected to a bank board position. Although she held an MBA and was an entrepreneur, she had far less industry experience than others on the board. She felt like she had to give intelligent answers even when she didn't have the context. Wanting to look competent, Regina participated only when she had a confident answer. Her colleagues rightfully questioned her level of authenticity. They thought she was aloof or wondered why she did not respond in the spirit of the question being asked.

Regina and I discussed how she was adjusting and she quickly relayed she felt out of her element. We talked about asking clarifying questions and using her "new kid on the block" card to ramp up with the help of her team members. Regina learned that she could be real and in doing so, she garnered more trust and respect. With the help of two colleagues she leaned into as teachers and guides, Regina let her guard down and went on to have a strong five-year run on the board.

When someone wears a glossy cover, it backfires. This can happen in professional settings when people have uneven levels of technical skills or industry knowledge, but it also happens when one person is more guarded and measured about what they don't know.

My family of origin taught me early on about wearing a glossy cover. To be fair, we were seen as a "high performing" family unit. The dynamic was more about achieving academic goals and displaying confidence and grace than about admitting what I didn't know or that I needed help. That said, my pleasing and over-achieving tendencies propelled me forward as a high-functioning executive. But, I wore this glossy cover of perfection well into adulthood.

As a successful career woman, I struggled with the demands of work and motherhood, and the weightiness of the end of my marriage. I'd put on my armor to go valiantly fight client battles, produce quality work, and achieve my targets on new business sales. Even though I was duly qualified, I always thought I had to "prove" myself. I also thought this quest necessitated me to be orderly, professional, unbiased, and maybe even a tad aloof to seem older and wiser. This routine left little room for spontaneity, flexibility and creativity – it was a "get 'er done" mentality.

One night after a lively project team dinner, a client commented that they enjoyed my sense of humor and off the cuff insights on their business that I shared over dinner. In the relaxed dinner environment, I had dropped my "must be polished and professional" demeanor and spoke from my heart. The client appreciated my candor and observations, and my genuineness.

This revelation made me wonder how much more of myself I could bring to my work and trust that my authenticity would not undermine my credibility. In recent years I have brought the frank, more vulnerable, spontaneously curious me to my consulting and coaching work, to great success. The key to this is wanting to be of service to others, and freeing myself to be instinctive, dance in the moment and bring my natural humor to bear. I've found this approach naturally beckons my clients to reveal more of themselves - and the business situation at hand becomes more of a puzzle on the table for us to solve together. As a personal aside, I've also brought more authenticity to my family, letting them see the real me, with emotions, hopes and quirkiness.

Imagine if you brought even fifty-percent more authenticity to work – and your team did too. What would that be like? Instead of snide comments and sarcasm, what if we all could be genuine and speak from the heart?

This "brave action" can feel like a risky endeavor. What if authenticity is not reciprocated or it turns the corner and becomes "honest criticism"? As a leader, you can start to reveal more authenticity in your workspace, judiciously of course. I've come to realize that the more I'm "me," the more energy I have and the more I can be of service.

From a practical standpoint, depending on your work environment, authenticity within the team can manifest in dramatically different ways. One of my clients is a Japanese pharmaceutical company, and their cultural climate focuses on calm demeanor and politeness at all costs. Therefore, even an ounce more of authenticity may be acknowledging when there is a difference of opinions and expressing desire to come to a solution. In contrast, an advertising agency with big personalities and big accounts on the line often yields fiery conversation about creative concepts and disagreements on what calls to make on a client account. Either way, the point is to bring "straight talk" and a degree of softness (not passiveness) to the conversation.

Here are some examples of how I teach my clients to approach a typical team meeting using markers of authenticity:

CREATE FOCUS AND SHARED UNDERSTANDING:

- Name the topic or issue you are solving for using familiar terms (not acronyms). State the facts at hand and what remains unresolved (why you are here in this meeting).

DEMONSTRATE THOUGHT LEADERSHIP:

- State your personal point of view on the topic. If you have a half-baked hypothesis, then own it and ask others to help bring more facts and ideas forward.

GET THE TEAM IN CONVERSATION:

- Encourage participation by pausing and asking if others have different thoughts.
- Ask for help and ideas, with a slight lean towards solution orientation, but not necessarily a hard answer.

MODEL STRAIGHT TALK:

- Use straight talk, being as specific and unveiled as you can be; no beating around the bush.

MAKE A DECISION, IF THE TIME IS RIGHT:

- Facilitate decision making if the conditions are right. This is an art, not a science. Elements can include presence of decision makers, reliability of data, resource allocation, and politics.

CLOSE THE MEETING:

- Know when the "arc" of the conversation has closed, or how to end precisely and not drag on. Provide a brief recap at the end of the meeting, and ask if points were missed.

Authenticity in your exchanges is directly related to trust and courage. Leadership Hero Code principles work together in tandem. In a psychologically safe environment, where the collective energy is positive and open, ideas are welcome. Team members are much more likely to step forward with "out of the box" ideas and musings, feeling free to be themselves. In addition, these same individuals are also more inclined to feel comfortable raising risks and concerns. This safe and authentic atmosphere contributes to the well-being of every member of the team.

RENEGADE JOINS CONSERVATIVE HEALTHCARE SYSTEM

What happens when an extroverted Italian self-made man who wears his emotions on his sleeve joins a conservative healthcare company? He lights it up! Michael joined this organization as the end cap to his illustrious career in advertising. When he first arrived, entire rooms of leaders would go speechless after he spoke because no one could believe his transparency and authenticity.

Michael said out loud that corporate shared services were underfunded and the company was losing market awareness and referrals because they were not keeping pace in advertising spend (e.g. losing share of voice). As a result, some people initially wrote him off as not a good cultural fit. This organization had a stellar reputation for delivering world-class care. How could it have problems and issues? However, Michael moved forward and assembled a new marketing team with hand-picked, highly specialized leaders and began to build a new brand and marketing strategy. His honesty was endearing with many, but it wasn't until he had a few wins on the board that some leaders began to take him seriously and engage in dialogue.

What did Michael model? He brought authenticity, created connection and made it safe to talk about the hard stuff. Three years into the leadership role, Michael still occasionally "gets excitable" when someone makes a corporate decision that impacts his team's plans and budgets. However, the trust he's built with physicians and colleagues, and his brand awareness metrics, can't be beat. Michael's model of authentic exchanges gives permission to all those around him to be more authentic and real in their interactions.

Keep in mind that authenticity is relative to your baseline personality. You do not take on a persona. You show up authentically as you. Doing so fuels others to do the same.

What do authentic exchanges look like for you today? What would one turn of the dial further towards authenticity look like? Trying to be "perfect" is never going to work. Being you, confidently, is the goal.

Intentional experiments in authenticity will give you a lot of information and feedback. In day-to-day team environments, it is quite easy to experiment and determine the impact because those individuals know the baseline you. However, I don't advise wild experimentation in a high stakes situation when you don't know the players. Master this skill with your inner circle of colleagues and primary teams first.

KEY TAKE-AWAYS:

- Authentic exchanges require an intention on your part – each and every day.

- These exchanges look different for different leadership styles and target audiences.

- As you practice greater levels of authenticity, you will be able to gauge the impact by the other person's eye contact, active listening and participation. Generally, the room will provide you with tangible and intangible feedback.

- What are you learning about your style of authentic exchange with others?

Write down a recent example of when you operated from true authenticity:

_____
_____
_____
_____
_____
_____ .

Now, write down an example of when you felt you held back some of your authenticity:

_____
_____
_____
_____
_____
_____ .

When you held back, how did you feel?
_____
_____
_____
_____
_____ .

"AUTHENTICITY IS A COLLECTION OF CHOICES WE HAVE TO MAKE EVERY DAY. IT'S ABOUT THE CHOICE TO SHOW UP AND BE REAL. THE CHOICE TO BE HONEST. THE CHOICE TO LET OUR TRUE SELVES BE SEEN."

— BRENÉ BROWN

CHAPTER 10:
TEAM LEADERSHIP HEALTH PRINCIPLE #4: VITAL CONVERSATIONS

We've explored the status of collective energy, psychological safety, and the presence of authentic exchanges in a team environment. These dimensions foreshadow the ability of the team to have deep and vital conversations.

If conversations are not feeling vital, perhaps it is because safety or authenticity is lacking. Of course, there are task-related conversations that are quite functional, so I am talking about the business-critical conversations that involve direction of resources, goals or strategies to support the business (or non-profit) at hand.

The nature of conversations within a team includes both formal and informal interactions, 1:1 conversation, and group conversations. Vital conversations start from the top. Take a moment to think about a team leader you've worked with recently. How do they bring themselves to conversations? To what degree are they open, frank, covering both concerns and "wins"? Do they use the lens of goals and objectives to guide conversation and make decisions?

While words definitely matter, the non-verbal cues and body language of interactions also impact the quality and productivity of these conversations. We often notice these silent signals in others, but do you seek to study yourself and how you come across?

When the first three team health indicators are favorable, the stage is set for honest and vital conversations, but sometimes we still can be on guard. Often, we think about what we should "add" or include in a conversation around an important topic. It is just as important to notice what we "delete" or do not include. Often these deletions are made to hasten decision making or stave off uncomfortable confrontation. When Leadership Hero Code fundamentals are at play, the team is willing and able to go to the necessary but uncomfortable places.

Statistics show that seventy percent of employees avoid difficult conversations with their boss, colleagues, and direct reports[13]. Whether it's due to the fear of retaliation, a negative effect on the relationship, or a lack of training, an overwhelming amount of people are avoiding tough conversations. This comes with considerable consequences. If the majority of employees are handling "toxic" situations by ignoring them, that will negatively impact business performance and communications, as well as individual and team well-being.

Take a moment to think through some vital conversations from your own perspective. Below is a worksheet that helps create awareness around patterns based on content, situation and personalities involved.

REFLECTIONS ON MY CONVERSATIONS	TOPIC	WHO WAS PRESENT?	WHAT QUALITIES DID THIS CONVERSATION HAVE?
Last work conversation that was challenging			
Last work conversation that was easy			
Where am I most direct and transparent?			
Where do my words differ from my body language?			
Where do I hold back or delete?			

What patterns did you find in this worksheet? You may find that certain topics or situations trigger a more or less vital set of conversations. Awareness is half the battle.

THE COURAGE TO ENGAGE IN VITAL CONVERSATIONS

Sharon was in charge of a 15-member strike team of data scientists and marketing professionals in a pharmaceutical company. The team had a four-year charter (and funding) to improve sales force call interactions with health professionals and customize interactions based on preferred methods of communications. The first year was a stealth year of development and infrastructure. The second year featured a mixed bag of some wins with proof of concepts, and some losses with data wonks interacting with the commercial operation. The third year was where the rubber met the road. As a Japanese-owned company, the cultural protocol called for polite interactions and indirect confrontation, but Sharon found herself in a coup-like situation.

The marketing division did an end-around and scheduled a customer journey summit to discuss the future of the team and whether or not the strike team should remain intact. Sharon realized that her "don't rock the boat" approach wasn't working in this setting. So, she prepared for a vital conversation with the head of marketing, Nico. Sharon was courageous enough to step forward and ask for a 1:1 in which she named the issue and asked for conversation first before gathering for a summit.

I worked with Sharon as this unfolded, urging her to consider what both teams might be able to align on in terms of capabilities needed for the future (regardless of leader). This left a question of "who" not "what or how." Sharon and Nico sat down and in the first meeting were able to agree on these two questions. Sharon decided to show her hand and ask Nico what alternatives he'd been contemplating as he thought about these goals and capabilities. And that's how the door was opened for conversation.

Nico truly believed the capabilities of artificial intelligence and machine learning were important – and his two main objections were 1) the capabilities were not scaling fast enough in his opinion

> and 2) he felt the customer journey team was not connected to his team and should be moved under his leadership. While it was a dramatic turn of events, Sharon uncovered the real motives and concerns. She tapped into vital conversations and sense of purpose to work together with Nico on possible scenarios. The real win here was diffusing a grand "summit" and moving towards a productive, leader to leader conversation.

After this scenario unfolded, I thought about the level of engagement within the organization and the degree to which employees felt they had a voice. Despite being a sophisticated $11B global pharmaceutical company, siloed teams and politics presented the ultimate opportunity to practice vital conversations. The ability to have vital conversations, and the need, exists in organizations of every size.

A study by Fierce Conversations and Quantum Workplace states, "Only about half of respondents said their conversations with colleagues or managers were 'excellent' or 'great'." The other half rated their conversations as 'less than great'. Engagement was higher among employees who rated conversations with coworkers and managers as great or excellent. Employees who rated conversations with coworkers as bad had a particularly low level of employee engagement."[14]

Once again, leadership effectiveness directly impacts employee engagement and we are here to improve in our role as leader every single day. These indicators are a great tool to keep you on track and in continual evaluation of how you and your team are doing.

Another way to examine vital conversations is to notice when a gap exists between one on one (1:1) conversation and what is communicated more broadly in team settings. Sometimes, due to title or perceived contribution, certain individuals receive less or different information than others, which can put them at a disadvantage.[15] More importantly, this lack of transparency with information is another constrictor that can cause people to take protective measures.

Let's do a well-being check on a team setting where you've witnessed a less than vital conversation.

TEAM MEETING (SELECT ONE FROM MEMORY)

TOPIC: _____

PLAYERS: _____

_____

COLLECTIVE ENERGY: _____

_____

VITAL CONVERSATIONS CHECKLIST

✓ Was the conversation or interaction meaningful and tangibly related to the business or mission?

✓ Was the actual topic or issue that prompted the exchange addressed?

✓ What were the deletions (or things not mentioned) in this conversation?

✓ Were words used to hint at things or convey underlying meaning?

✓ Were any clarifying questions asked during this conversation?

✓ What was the quality of listening in the room?

Going forward, what can you do differently to facilitate vital conversations? We've talked a lot about the team ecosystem and what happens when conversations are not vital or crucial enough, but it can't be overstated that you need to examine how you are contributing to quality conversations or detracting from them. My challenge to you is to identify where you are avoiding a challenging conversation.

KEY TAKE-AWAYS:

- Vital conversations are a regular part of a heathy team biome; they aren't always easy and often require bravery.

- You are responsible for contributing to the ecosystem by engaging in vital conversations on a regular basis; start where the stakes are low and work your way up.

- There is usually one leader in your world who models positive conversational behavior; study them and determine what methods might suit your style.

What are you learning about vital conversations and how you engage in them? One of the most useful tips is to create awareness of what is unsaid and how that impacts the work environment. The "hold backs" can often do more damage than the big knock-down-drag-out fights.

Write down one area where a vital conversation has been brewing – but you haven't started the dialogue yet:

_____
_____
_____
_____
_____ .

What is holding you back from having this conversation?

_____
_____
_____
_____ .

"AT THE EXECUTIVE AND MANAGERIAL LEVELS, WORK IS ALMOST ALWAYS CONVERSATION IN ONE FORM OR ANOTHER, AND YET WE SPEND ALMOST NO TIME APPRENTICING OURSELVES TO THE DISCIPLINES NECESSARY FOR HOLDING REAL EXCHANGES. THAT'S PARTLY BECAUSE THEY INVOLVE A GREAT DEAL OF SELF-KNOWLEDGE AND A WILLINGNESS TO STUDY HOW HUMAN BEINGS TRY TO BELONG — SKILLS WE HOPE OUR STRATEGIC ABILITIES WILL HELP US GET BY WITHOUT."

DAVID WHYTE

CHAPTER 11:
LINKING LEADERSHIP PRINCIPLES TO PURPOSE

If your team indexes positively on the four leadership principles just reviewed, and yet you don't have an articulated purpose to guide the team, you will still struggle to achieve performance and engagement goals. The job of a leader is to clearly verbalize the vision, main objectives, and metrics. In a nutshell, when it comes to understanding purpose, you can simply ask: Are we all marching in the same direction and do we know why?

Frankly, regardless of role or title, you can contribute to a clearer purpose.

Human nature craves to know why we do what we do, and knowing the reason and intent of any particular project or task is especially important in the workplace. If you have ever been around a two-year-old, you know they have no trouble asking why (over and over). As adults in our careers, we too need to understand why and want to know where our piece fits in the overarching puzzle. But we sometimes hesitate to ask.

How do you know if your team has "a purpose"?

USE THIS CHECKLIST:

✓ Actual, documented goal and objectives

✓ Key initiatives or priorities (outlined and clear to all)

✓ Budget and resource allocations discussed and agreed upon

✓ Decisions that impact business direction or resources cascaded in a timely manner from leader to manager to staff

✓ R-A-C-I (responsible, accountable, consulted, informed) roles and accountabilities outlined

In my experience, it is a rare team that operates with all of these elements in place. More often than not, I will join a client with the stated purpose of optimizing their marketing operations, growing market share, or to help execute on an unusually complex initiative, only to find that there isn't a clear strategic plan that is on paper, understood and agreed upon, assigned to responsible individuals, and with clear metrics. Whew, that was a lot to ask for. Here is an example of a high performing team.

MAINTAINING FOCUS THROUGH A MERGER

Christel is SVP Marketing for a 10-hospital system merging with 7-hospital system. Two systems were in discussions to merge and create a consolidated, high-performing marketing function. One had an annual set of brand goals, the other operated based on physician and administrator needs "on demand." For a variety of reasons, Christel was installed as the new CMO for the merged system. She recognized a need to honor legacy teams but also create an annual, integrated marketing and communications plan. This was urgent, to support each hospital president and region in the new system.

Her ability to be authentic, create safety, and provide tangible vision and goals made Christel a rock star and created an atmosphere where all involved, at all levels, were completely comfortable asking questions and pointing out things that were missing from the vision and goals.

Christel truly integrated critical behaviors that built trust in parallel with vision setting. Importantly, the marketing team was able to build brand awareness of the new combined entity, and increase market share for specific service lines within the first eighteen months of the merger. This speaks to the power of effective leadership and trust. Christel was able to build this not only with the executive team but also with her whole department.

No matter the stakes, large or small, long-term or short-term, the team needs to be clear on the charter. As a leader who embodies the Leadership Hero Code, you can make this easier for all.

Below are tried and true checklists for when a team or leader is operating "on purpose." These directives reflect both behaviors and skills that are healthy in a team setting.

LEADERS OPERATING ON PURPOSE

- ✓ Identify and articulate system and/or regional goals
- ✓ Socialize these goals with other leaders
- ✓ Negotiate key partner functions/contributions
- ✓ Articulate metrics using the CEO/system-familiar measures
- ✓ Activate the team against these goals and realities

LEADERSHIP TEAMS OPERATING ON PURPOSE

- ✓ Shape their teams around the goals and initiatives
- ✓ Discuss trade-offs with peers to achieve goals
- ✓ Establish budget parameters
- ✓ Provide updates on real-time progress or barriers
- ✓ Request information from one-ups that can aid the staff or teams in doing their jobs

STAFF OPERATING ON PURPOSE

- ✓ Able to confidently speak to their individual responsibilities
- ✓ Converse regularly with their manager and peers about their work and how it intersects with other teams

- ✓ Ask clarifying questions
- ✓ "Manage up" when asked about a peer or manager (not negative speak)

Can you tell I am passionate about operating with a clear mandate? I trust you are too. That said, not every leader can capture and articulate their vision. Recently, I came across a leader who is beloved, inspirational, and visionary, yet not a natural whiz at PowerPoint, developing diagrams and plans that all link together coherently and cohesively. We worked to capture their words and concepts in a shareable format to share with the team and staff. Being an effective leader is not about being all things to all people, it is being the best you, boldly and confidently.

The Leadership Hero Code is a means to that end. The well-being checks provided here are for you to apply to your current situation and continually as your career evolves. Being a "hero" in your own life means you know why you get dressed and go to work every day, and you bring your A-game to inspire those around you.

Being a contributor is the heart and soul of what we do. The principles of the Leadership Hero Code all have this unwavering sense of belonging and contribution as the bullseye. When everyone understands the function and expectation of their efforts, communication flows more freely and employee engagement and job satisfaction elevate.

KEY TAKE-AWAYS:

The backbone of any team is the degree to which scope and priorities are clear and people understand how they contribute to the broader team and organization.

The hat trick of leadership is when a team has an articulated set of goals, leadership skills (aptitude), and positive collective energy (attitude); do not fear if your team indexes higher in one area over another.

You can help shape and clarify the charter from any seat; it is how you go about this clarification that matters and with whom you engage.

What are you learning about your sense of purpose and how it aligns with overall team sense of purpose? What is one area you intuitively know you need to clarify for your own role?

"WHEN LEADERS LACK A CLEAR VISION OF THE GROUP'S FUTURE, THEY ARE FEELING THEIR WAY THROUGH THE EXECUTION PROCESS, RELYING ON DAY-TO-DAY REVELATIONS. SURE, THEY HAVE A COLLECTION OF GOALS, PLANS AND SCHEDULES, BUT THEY DON'T SEE THE UNDERLYING TAPESTRY, HOW EVERYTHING FITS TOGETHER."

THE WORK OF LEADERS

CHAPTER 12:
INTEGRATING PERSONAL AND TEAM LEADERSHIP PRINCIPLES

You have now completed a well-being checkup using seven leadership health indicators across individual and team domains and linked these to the importance of clear strategy and goals. Now we will turn towards integrating these practices into your day-to-day work life.

In the more than two dozen seminal leadership models presented over the past two decades, the common thread is the exponential power of individually effective leaders who skillfully work together towards a common purpose, with shared vocabulary, and a tolerance for discomfort. The Leadership Hero Code model reflects these global learnings, and focuses in on specific dimensions of leadership health that can serve first as diagnostics, and then as opportunities for change and growth.

Let's look at the interplay between individual and team leadership health principles. How do you react when one of the four indicators in the team environment goes askew and impacts your individual work? Likewise, what do you proactively bring to the team environment when you sense it is needed?

Integration of the individual and team leadership principles is about becoming aware of your energy, your impact, and how you intentionally shift to influence the team ecosystem. The goal is to use your awareness of these principles to make deliberate choices and move from being a participant to authoring a more courageous and energized set of conversations in the workplace. You are in the driver's seat. You are a leader who can make a difference in your own quality of life and others as well.

Ironic but true, many organizations that specialize in leadership or communications forget to ask for feedback on their own leadership effectiveness. One client of mine stepped forward courageously to solicit feedback from every member of the firm and identify improvements.

THE COBBLER'S SHOE

A global business communications training firm discovered that after three decades of growth and success in the marketplace, their employees felt that inclusivity and vital communications were at risk. In fact, employees stated that they wanted to provide structured feedback to the leadership team but did not feel comfortable. As a result, the firm reached out to me to conduct a 360-leadership assessment, seeking input from all levels of the organization on the seven leaders. Now, the irony of this is not lost on me (or you).

In the pre-planning stages, I talked with the individual leaders about these indicators – how was their energy bank, sense of purpose, and attention to self-care? What I found was that energy was low given all the demands on each leader, sense of purpose was clear to each individual but not consistent across the leadership team, and self-care efforts were slim. The cycles of client delivery and hitting sales targets had left them in a state of perpetual motion, with limited reflection or ideation time.

The main theme we uncovered was that the "formula" that made the firm successful for several decades didn't feel like the most productive path forward given the advent of social media, virtual work teams, and agile project approaches. A new mandate was needed to equip the team with confidence and skill sets to navigate change on behalf of their clients and adapt older communication models to fit the client's unique needs.

As a first step, I worked with the executive team to solicit structured 360 feedback to ensure team members across parts of the organization could provide input. Then, I worked with each executive to understand their aggregate 360 results – statistical scores and write-in comments. Lastly, I developed a "group report" for the leadership team that highlighted the principal themes in terms of constructive feedback. This set of data-based insights was a bit of an eye-opener for the leadership team. Scores were low in some key areas of courageous authenticity and collaboration. However, the feedback informed the next generation direction and behaviors for the team. The entire organization reviewed high level results and implications and had robust tabletop discussions about purpose and the nature of vital conversations.

Truly powerful leaders are interested in giving and receiving constructive criticism. Elon Musk, for example, believes that "you have to actively pursue negative feedback from the people around you. I spend a small amount of my time on good news, but I pay attention to the bad news."[16] The spirit of Elon's thinking is worth highlight, though I don't encourage seeking only "bad news." Thoughtful and candid feedback, positive and negative, plays an important role in improving leadership effectiveness, as does "voice of the customer" research.

REVOLUTIONIZING A NOT-FOR-PROFIT

There has been a significant migration of corporate leaders into not-for-profit roles that fulfill a personal sense of purpose and mission. I was delighted to work with the nation's largest domestic hunger-relief agency during a time of tremendous organizational change. A new CEO and new Chief Marketing Officer were on board and wanted to chart a new course with a more contemporary brand and donor engagement strategy. The new CMO, Will, had significant experience in brand strategy, segmentation, and campaign development. As we set out to interview key stakeholders and define the donor research needs, we were met with immediate resistance. Why change what has "been working" for twenty years? The collective energy was like molasses.

However, we set out to learn from existing and prospective donors how they perceive the organization, the cause of hunger in the United States, and how they make decisions about where to donate. We also examined the agency's database and the existing data fields to best understand the profile of their current donor base. The eye-opening moment came in sharing the research findings. Donors and prospective donors didn't understand the role the umbrella organization played in relation to local food banks, and more importantly, they didn't understand the depth of the hunger crisis in America. These were "aha" moments that Will and I shared, backed by data.

We provided clips of the focus groups so leaders of different teams could witness the voices of the donors. As reality began to sink in for legacy leaders of the organization, we engaged them in conversation about meeting donor needs from a different perspective. These conversations were both glorious and arduous and required authentic exchanges and psychological safety left and right. However, this leaning into the discomfort helped shift all parties toward contributing to shared meaning and direction. The team mobilized to develop a set of recommendations and began the process of vetting and prioritizing with leaders.

Among other business operations improvements, Will led the charge to develop an awareness campaign that focused on the issue (1 in 6 don't know where their next meal will come from) and an educational campaign that highlighted what the national organization does in conjunction with local food banks. Clarity of purpose was the true win. The re-launched, contemporary brand look implemented was just icing on the cake.

One of the biggest learnings from working with teams on change initiatives or transformation projects is to engage leaders in conversation about their aspirations for the customer or end user and their perceived leadership contributions. You may have been mentored early on to focus on "what's in it for me?" (WIFM). However, giving, and being recognized by team members for that contribution, is a major source of engagement and trust. As Jeremy Scrivens, an HR consultant and thought leader, shared in an interview, "I have learned that people are more motivated by what they can give than by what they can get. Yet for years we have engaged people the other way around."[17] What does all this focus on feedback mean for you? The willingness to give feedback in earnest is just as important as the openness to receiving feedback and contemplating change. The most impressive and competent leaders are those who have a sincere focus on the mission, understand their own leadership strengths and weaknesses, and have the capability to interact with other leaders in ambiguous, complex and unpredictable situations. This broader sense of leadership capability and agility is what you are able to embody going forward.

As you integrate these Leadership Hero Code principles and practices for yourself personally and for your team, inspiration and courage will grow and thrive. You can bust through status quo and myths and the old way of doing business as usual. Fulfillment, satisfaction, curiosity, and mutual appreciation can become your new norm.

"WHEN WE CHOOSE TO BE RESPONSIBLE AND CREATIVE RATHER THAN REACTIVE, WE STOP BEING VICTIMS OF OUR LIFE… THE CHOICE OF RESPONSIBILITY PUTS US SQUARELY IN THE DRIVER'S SEAT OF OUR LIFE. LEADERSHIP DEVELOPMENT, THEN, BECOMES ABOUT GROWING THE SIZE OF THE WORLD FOR WHICH ONE IS ABLE TO BE RESPONSIBLE."

KAREN AND HENRY KIMSEY-HOUSE

CHAPTER 13:
MOVING YOUR TEAM INTO ACTION

While you can and should experiment with your own individual leadership behaviors, a different approach is required to engage a team of people in change efforts. The four team principles laid out here are practiced attitudes and behaviors that contribute to a healthy team ecosystem. The pivot point is your decision to show up with courageous authenticity.

To move your team into action, the first step is to examine how you personally impact or contribute to collective energy, psychological safety, authentic exchanges, and vital conversations. As one wise mentor said to me: look in the mirror first. I do these well-being checks myself and based on experiments over time, I know my strengths and where I need more focus.

For example, I know that I can influence vital conversations in a group setting. One way I do that is to notice the collective energy and use that to create openings for vital conversations. In one situation, I worked with a leadership team that was tasked with fundraising $150M over a three-year period for a new stand-alone facility on top of the fundraising targets they already had in place. The collective energy in the room was a state of overwhelm and fatigue. I simply named it out loud. "As I look around the room today, I can see the weight on your shoulders…."

This naming created an opening to systematically approach the enormous task at hand and begin to talk about the questions, the opportunities, the worries. We began to engage in vital conversations about the existing workload and expectations for the team. The core of the matter was, "how are other leaders helping to raise funds so we are not alone?". One of the recommendations I made was to create a Steering Committee for this initiative to coordinate efforts and share information to create visibility and accountability for fundraising, together. Creating community and structure around transformational projects is critical. The task is easier to do when you incorporate the leadership principles laid out here.

Hopefully you have one in mind that you might consider your "superpower," or at least a skill you can pull like an arrow from its quiver. Some leaders like the tangibility of creating a clear purpose and set out on a path to lay out the "why" and then layer in the "what" (goods or services we deliver) and then the "how" (unique methods, capabilities).

As you have been reading, have any of the skills resonated within you more strongly or you recognized that you are competent in that area, or perhaps need more focus there? Do you feel clarity of purpose?

Frequently when I am brought in for consultant work, I find that teams often have some "hot" projects, but in reality, there is not widespread clarity on the top 3-5 objectives or goals and how each part of the team is contributing to (and accountable for) the bigger picture. Further, the "why" behind the team's focus areas or the organization's overall strategic ambition is not clear to many leaders, let alone front-line staff. What happens then? Individuals who don't have clear line of sight will often make up their own set of priorities. This can create silos and duplicative work.

If there is only one initiative you can spearhead for your team, it would be to facilitate this very conversation. In fact, I would directly ask your team: What is the highest and best use we can organize our team around, for the sake of the customer and a healthy leadership ecosystem?

Your leadership intention is the most important element. You can make a difference as an individual, high-performing leader – and even more of a difference in partnership with team members to create a work environment and sense of purpose that calls each of you to a higher ground, without heroics or exhaustion.

Being a true leadership hero means you are able to sustain, and enjoy, your career.

There is no longer a status quo. Let's work together to create a new, dynamic work environment that is built upon trust, agility and courage. One of my life's greatest joys is seeing great teamwork come to fruition, guided by a clear sense of purpose. This satisfaction can become part of your daily work life.

THE NEEDLE CAN MOVE

> I received a call from a regular client, Jackson, who wanted to update me that his leadership team moved forward with the strategic plan and priority projects we identified together and metrics are looking really positive – they are regaining market share. Their engagement scores for the team went up, two low performing employees moved on and were replaced with complementary talent. Then Jackson said, "I didn't really know if this was going to work, but we've really made a turnaround. Remember when you told me I could be my own leadership hero and serve the greater good of the team? I think we're in the sweet spot."

If you are an exhausted over-performer and find yourself grinding away in your current work environment, now is the time to move forward and actively create "the sweet spot." You now have access to different levers for your individual leadership and how you approach your team.

Many of my clients are lifetime overachievers, driven to perform and also subject to fatigue. Sometimes they are on the cliff of burnout as they engage with me to develop a strategic plan or turnaround initiative. As they begin to adopt new behaviors and actively construct their workdays, they see a clearer path forward and have more energy and focus. This is what is possible for you. As a fellow human and leader in today's tumultuous times, recognize this as a call to action to courageously examine what's possible and make it happen.

I didn't always employ this code. Earlier in my career, I too was caught up in the pressure cooker of success. I vividly recall one late evening as my head bobbed slightly due to fatigue, but I worked hard to keep my wits about me as Bob, the head of data architecture, said we may not be able to "go live" as promised. At 2am, the whole team was on the conference line or in the war room. We were preparing to finally launch an entirely new website and content management system for a large, nationally recognized health system. I'd been working 17-hour days for more than nine months, carrying three director's roles. This was a big moment. If we could launch successfully, then the team would triumph and I may have some relief and time off!

With a deep breath, I said to Bob, "I am not willing to let this go until tomorrow. To be clear, what you're telling me is that we have 5,000 physician profiles loaded and somehow 300 show their office is located in the middle of the Atlantic Ocean?"

Bob thought there was a bug in the data feed impacting geolocation accuracy. I directed Bob to sit with another team member and review code line by line. At 4am, post-bug fix and reboot, it appeared as though profile locations were accurate. Just to be safe, we ran one more test and review of code. Now it was completely up to me. I decided it was a go – we'd been waiting eagerly as an organization to have a mobile-friendly, dynamic website designed for patients and researchers. I sent a quick note to the CEO who was anticipating the launch, and got back a thumbs up.

Forty-eight hours later, the phones started ringing. Physicians were looking themselves up online and their specialties and clinical interests were not what they remembered. We reminded the doctors that the medical staff office owned the credentials database and we simply fed off that database. It became quite clear that these physicians had not looked at their listing data for many years. While this wasn't our responsibility in marketing, it was now seen as a "website problem" that must be rectified.

We'd recognized all along that specialties and interests varied quite a bit between hospitals acquired over the years, but didn't see that as a problem we could solve for in Phase 1 of a new website. Unfortunately, the CEO was more than displeased with the physicians knocking on his door. All the good features, contemporary design and enriched content and interface were not recognized. Instead of a shining triumph, the project felt like a huge failure for me.

Over the course of the next month, we logged 107 meetings with physicians and had several sessions with the medical staff office to make that fix. On the bright side, statistics showed greater conversion for making appointments online and downloads of articles in exchange for email addresses. I was exhausted. I'd given so much of my time and energy to this initiative and what I learned from leading this eight-million-dollar project (that is now driving forty percent more appointments booked online) is invaluable. I had ignored my own dipping energy bank and lack of self-care in the name of the higher purpose and glory of the first new website for this large enterprise. Why on earth did I attempt to be a superhero and cover multiple director roles while also launching a new website? I did not have a heart attack but that was my wake-up call.

Being a "hero" has a whole new meaning for me now. And why I, too, need to keep these Leadership Hero Code principles front and center. Not surprisingly, I apply them in my personal life as well.

Let's circle back to the beginning. Your personal health, including your sleep, is influenced by your workplace. So is your confidence, mindset, and sense of stability. Your entire well-being is impacted by the dynamics in your work environment and the meetings you participate in day in and day out. If the workplace is construed as a "contagious" environment, implementing the Leadership Hero Code is how you build up your immunity. You can do more than survive, you can thrive. You can create a more rewarding work culture so the influence and effect the environment has is not harmful or stressful. You can bring what you have learned here to create a new culture, one in which you can grow, flourish, and blossom. You can be a catalyst for your team and create a new way, a much healthier and fulfilling way, of doing business as usual. Together, we can create this new norm.

My sincere wish is that the Leadership Hero Code helps you have more vitality and engagement in your teams, in your career, and your life.

I invite you to share your experiments, stories and learnings in our online community. You can find printable worksheets and tools at www.leadershipherocode.com.

Thank you for reading and joining me on the journey.

"THE LEADERS WHO EMBRACE AN INFINITE MINDSET... BUILD STRONGER, MORE INNOVATIVE, MORE INSPIRING ORGANIZATIONS. THEIR PEOPLE TRUST EACH OTHER AND THEIR LEADERS. THEY HAVE THE RESILIENCE TO THRIVE IN AN EVER-CHANGING WORLD, WHILE THEIR COMPETITORS FALL BY THE WAYSIDE. ULTIMATELY, THEY ARE THE ONES WHO LEAD THE REST OF US INTO THE FUTURE. ANY WORTHWHILE UNDERTAKING STARTS WITH WHY — THE PURPOSE, CAUSE OR BELIEF THAT INSPIRES US TO DO WHAT WE DO AND INSPIRES OTHERS TO JOIN US."

SIMON SINEK

BONUS EXPERIMENTS

Being your own hero means taking brave actions, and those are unique to each individual. Hopefully, you have an intuitive sense of how you might spark a conversation or boldly step forward to speak your mind authentically. Whether you are a bellwether or a change agent, go forth. If this all seems daunting, step back and engage in some of the awareness practices to bring more information and insight to your own reactions in the workplace.

SAMPLE AWARENESS EXPERIMENTS:

- In an upcoming team meeting, notice how the chair or lead for the meeting introduces the agenda and purpose of the meeting.

- As your department or team leader interacts with you, how do they reference business goals and why you are "doing what you are doing"?

- Where do you notice siloes of information that could be causing distraction, anxiousness or duplication of efforts?

SAMPLE ENERGY BANK EXPERIMENT:

- Take this next week to notice how you feel at work overall.

- What excited you and added to your energy bank?

- What or who depleted you? Why?

- What would help you move your role or focus towards the energy-giving activities?
- How could you use your voice and point of view (body language, intonation) to address the depleting areas?

SAMPLE SENSE OF PURPOSE EXPERIMENT:

As it relates to living and leading on purpose, the best way to look at this is with fresh eyes. What have you been asked to "do" in work and in life? Sometimes this is your actual job description or a conversation with someone. Write down what you believe your objectives and focus areas truly are.

My role at _____ is to

_____

Because_____

_____

I'll do this by _____

_____

Now, take stock in what you've written down – how clear do you feel about your own leadership charter or purpose? Have a scheduled conversation about this to check in on expectations and also confirm the priorities you have set as a leader.

SAMPLE INVESTIGATION OF THE "WHY" EXPERIMENT:

Uncovering and articulating the "why" behind the team mission is one of the most worthwhile conversations to invest in. Communication and conversational skills are an integral part of creating alignment around purpose — and it might be messy. There may be a role model leader or director within the team that regularly displays the skills below:

✓ Uses precise language to describe the problem, the facts and the solution

✓ Demonstrates active listening in group meetings
✓ Ties all work to the objectives of broader organization
✓ Asks relevant, clarifying questions to create shared understanding and scope
✓ Focuses on the known needs of the end-user or customer

This role model can be a good ally and help design some guiding precepts for conversation within the leadership team. Most often, it helps to have an objective facilitator or moderator help shape some of these activities (e.g. plan frameworks, due dates) in parallel with the strategic planning process native to the organization.

This may all sound ridiculously simple. And yet, with business as usual, creating structured space dedicated to purpose is not all that easy. The process and approach I offer is not to bring rigidity and formality, but to help set the table for productive conversations.

SAMPLE CONVERSATION-FOCUSING EXPERIMENT:

In planning meetings, people will stray to talk about hot business issues. You can use some of these approaches to keep the conversation on track:

What we are trying to accomplish is an agreed-upon purpose or vision statement that serves as the north star for our initiatives, resource allocation and metrics.

- Some hypotheses on our vision are… (gather input)

- Some hypotheses on our top 3 objectives… (gather input)

- How would you prioritize these objectives for our team?

- What are the decisions that need to be made (now or shortly)?

- I'm noting your idea here in the "parking lot" for now so that we can stay focused (great way to capture ideas that are adjacent or non-related).

END NOTES

[1] "Hemingway's Hero and Code Hero." *EnglishLiterature.Net*, 20 Jan. 2019, http://englishliterature.net/notes/hemingways-hero-and-code-hero.

[2] Pfeffer, Jeffrey. *Dying for a Paycheck: Why the American Way of Business Is Injurious to People and Companies.* HarperCollins Publishers, 2018.

[3] "Mental Health in the Workplace." *World Health Organization*, World Health Organization, 9 Aug. 2019, https://www.who.int/mental_health/in_the_workplace/en/.

[4] "Workplace Wellness Report: Mind the Workplace." Mental Health America. 2019.

[5] "Stop the Meeting Madness." *Harvard Business Review*, July 2017. [6]"Workplace Wellness Report: [6]Mind the Workplace." Mental Health America. 2019.

[6] "Workplace Wellness Report: Mind the Workplace." Mental Health America. 2019.

[7] "Change Management: Managing Organizational Change." *Gartner*, Sept. 2018, https://www.gartner.com/en/insights/change-management.

8 "Chapter 2: Leadership Effectiveness and Business Performance." *Mastering Leadership: an Integrated Framework for Breakthrough Performance and Extraordinary Business Results*, by Robert J. Anderson and William A. Adams, Wiley, 2016, pp. 13–25.

9 Brown, Gregory Scott. "Why Men Are Falling in Love With Self-Care." *Psychology Today*, Sussex Publishers, May 2019, www.psychologytoday.com/us/blog/green-psychiatry/201905/why-men-are-falling-in-love-self-care.

10 Neff, Kristin. *Self-Compassion: Stop Beating Yourself up and Leave Insecurity Behind*. William Morrow, 2015.

11 Brar, Faith. "Self-Care Is More Important to Millennial Women Than Ever Before." *Shape*, www.shape.com/lifestyle/mind-and-body/more-half-millenial-women-made-self-care-their-new-years-resolution-2018.

12 "Workplace Wellness Report: Mind the Workplace." Mental Health America. 2019.

13 Schneider, Michael. "Most People Handle Difficult Situations by Ignoring Them -- and the Fallout Isn't Pretty." *Inc.com*, Inc., 22 Aug. 2018, www.inc.com/michael-schneider/70-percent-of-employees-avoid-difficult-conversations-their-companies-are-suffering-as-a-result.html.

14 Workplace, Quantum. "6 Insights on Effective Workplace Communication, Fierce Conversations, and Miscommunication." *6 Insights on Effective Workplace Communication, Fierce Conversations, and Miscommunication*, 2019, www.quantumworkplace.com/fierce-conversations-effective-workplace-communication-miscommunication.

15 "Workplace Wellness Report: Mind the Workplace." Mental Health America. 2019.

[16]Boog, Jason. "Elon Musk: 'Pay Attention to Negative Feedback, and Solicit It, Particularly from Friends.'" Adweek, 21 Mar. 2013, www.adweek.com/digital/elon-musk-pay-attention-to-negative-feedback-and-solicit-it-particularly-from-friends/.

[17]Brownsey, Kevin, et al. "Appreciative Inquiry to Build a Culture of Kindness." *Leadership & Change Magazine,* 17 Nov. 2015, www.leadershipandchangemagazine.com/appreciative-inquiry-to-build-a-culture-of-kindness/.

ABOUT THE AUTHOR

Kristen Hemingway is a veteran strategist and team leadership coach, on a mission to create skilled leaders who generate and demand positive change. Kristen builds off the Hemingway family legacy with a twist on Ernest's literary Code Hero to address today's leader – offering courageous skill-building to shift how you and your teams operate together in change-filled times. She works with Fortune 500 companies, not-for-profit organizations and innovators across a range of industries. Visit www.hemingwaystrategies.com for content, workbooks and ideas for fueling your leadership.

www.ingramcontent.com/pod-product-compliance
Lightning Source LLC
Chambersburg PA
CBHW050302010526
44108CB00040B/2163